THE DIAGRAM GROUP

FUNKY FACTS

STERLING PUBLISHING CO., INC.

NEW YORK

Library of Congress Cataloging-in-Publication Data Available

1   3   5   7   9   10   8   6   4   2

Published by Sterling Publishing Company, Inc.
387 Park Avenue South, New York, N.Y. 10016
A Diagram Book first created by Diagram Visual Information Limited
195 Kentish Town Road, London NW5 8SY, England
© 1996 by Diagram Visual Limited
Distributed in Canada by Sterling Publishing
% Canadian Manda Group, One Atlantic Avenue, Suite 105
Toronto, Ontario, Canada M6K 3E7
Distributed in Australia by Capricorn Link (Australia) Pty Ltd.
P.O. Box 6651, Baulkham Hills, Business Centre, NSW 2153, Australia

Sterling ISBN 0-8069-8124-5

The most snow to fall in one storm in the United States fell at Mt. Shasta Ski Bowl in California, in February 1959. The storm lasted for seven days, and 189 inches (4.8m) of snow was recorded – enough to bury a small house.

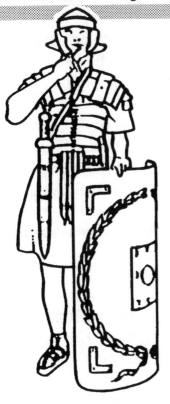

Tasty toothpaste

The first recorded use of toothpaste was about a thousand years ago by a Roman called Scibonius Largus. It was a mixture of honey, salt, and ground glass. Ancient Spaniards dipped their toothbrushes in human urine.

The first robots

The word "robot" comes from the Czech word "robota," which means "forced work." It was used in a play by Karel Capek, called *Rossum's Universal Robots*, which was performed in London in 1923. The first robots appeared in stories as mechanical men which obeyed orders without question. Today, robots are machines which are programmed to carry out certain types of work automatically.

The purity of gold is measured in carats. The top rate of purity is 24 carats, but this is too soft for most jewelry. A common rate is 18 carats – which is three-quarters pure.

Dressed crabs

Spider crabs like dressing up in disguise so much they let other creatures build homes on their backs. These crabs are quite common, but they are difficult to see because they look so much like the seabed.

Losing weight

If you stand on the scales at the Equator, you will weigh less than at the North Pole. This is because the Equator is farther from Earth's center, and the pull of gravity is less.

A queen termite spends her life in the nest, laying eggs. She is fed by worker termites a hundred times smaller than she is. The queen lays as many as 1,000 eggs a day. When she stops producing eggs, she is starved to death.

Walking tall

Did you know that you are taller in the morning than at night? This is because you have soft pads (called disks) between the bones of your spine. They expand slightly overnight, making you taller.

Life and death

The Colosseum in ancient Rome was an arena where people could watch gladiators fight. When gladiators fought each other, the loser died, but the winner was allowed to live.

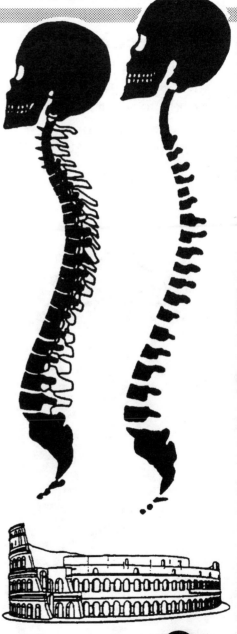

The highest temperature ever officially recorded in the United States was in well-named Death Valley, California, in July 1913. There, about 175 feet (53.3m) below sea level, the thermometer reached 134°F (56.7°C).

Supercharged

Nerve impulses carry messages from your body to your brain at speeds of up to 180 mph (289.6km) – the top speed of a fast car.

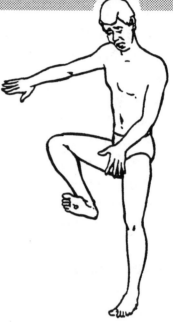

Male mother

A male sea horse has a special pouch on its stomach. The female sea horse lays her eggs in it. The eggs are fertilized and develop in the pouch until they are big enough to be born. Then the male goes into labor and gives birth, pushing the babies out into the sea.

The snake that poisons the most people each year is the king cobra, which lives in India. It has even been known to kill elephants by driving its fangs into the soft tip of the animal's trunk.

Smallest state

Vatican City in Italy is the world's smallest state – less than one-quarter square mile (.6 sq km). Only about 1,000 people live there. It prints its own stamps and money.

The first teddy bears

In 1902, President Theodore "Teddy" Roosevelt, on a hunting trip, refused to shoot a bear cub. The story was printed in the *Washington Post* with a cartoon. A storekeeper cashed in on the story by making toy bears which he called "Teddy's bears."

The Grand Canyon in Arizona is 280 miles (450.6km) long, 1 mile (1.6km) deep, and up to 18 miles (28.9km) across. It was carved out by the Colorado River and took about 10,000,000 million years to get to its present size.

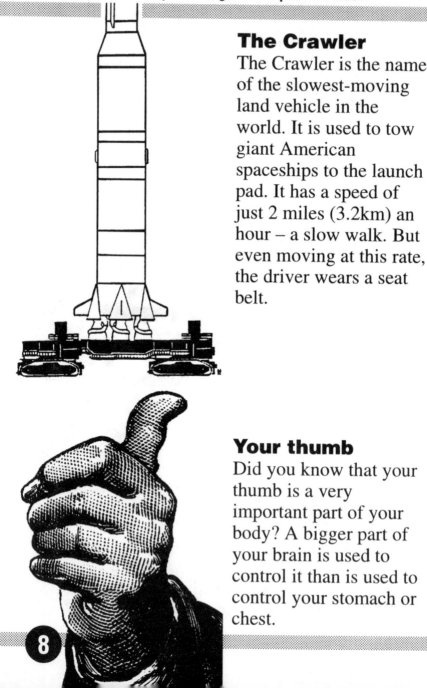

The Crawler

The Crawler is the name of the slowest-moving land vehicle in the world. It is used to tow giant American spaceships to the launch pad. It has a speed of just 2 miles (3.2km) an hour – a slow walk. But even moving at this rate, the driver wears a seat belt.

Your thumb

Did you know that your thumb is a very important part of your body? A bigger part of your brain is used to control it than is used to control your stomach or chest.

The first car had a steam engine and was driven by a Frenchman, Nicholas Cugnot, in 1769. On his first outing he had the world's first car accident, and a year later he was jailed as the first dangerous driver.

Amazing acorns

This is the actual size of an acorn. It can grow into a tree 120 feet (36.5m) high.

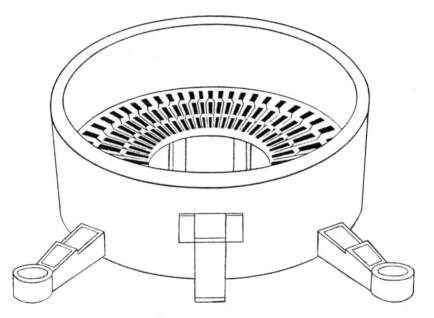

Towers of silence

If you belonged to the ancient religion called Zoroastrianism, you would know about its strange way of dealing with its dead. The Zoroastrians, who live in northern India and Iran, put their dead on platforms, known as Towers of Silence. These round towers are built on high ground so that the bodies, open to the air, can be eaten by vultures.

The most expensive hurricane in the United States was Hurricane Andrew, which hit the Gulf Coast in August 1992. It is reckoned to have caused more than $20 billion worth of damage in South Florida.

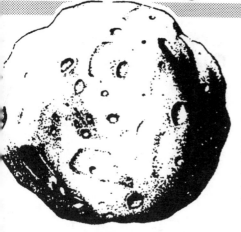

Bomb blast
Some people think the dinosaurs died out because of a meteor. This stone – 6 miles (9.6 km) wide – from space hit Earth 65 million years ago.

Fight to the death
Many years ago, two gentlemen settled their arguments with sword fights, or duels, and often died. Duels are now banned everywhere except in Uruguay – as long as the duelists are blood donors.

A sow and her six piglets were sentenced to death for eating a child in France in 1547. The sow was killed, but the piglets were allowed to live because of their youth and the bad example set by their mother.

With a kiss

Kissing has not always meant love. The ancient Romans kissed someone on the mouth or eyes as a greeting. And for centuries, kissing a hand, foot, or the ground a person walked on was a sign of respect.

Mouthful

Some of the dinosaurs that ate other dinosaurs had huge back legs but very small front ones. What they used their front legs for is a puzzle. The legs were too short for pushing food into the dinosaurs' mouths.

The largest reptile in the sea is the Pacific leatherback turtle. It grows up to 7 feet (2.1m) long and weighs nearly 1,000 lb (453.6kg) – more than the weight of five large men.

How many Chinese?

China has more people than any other country – 1,158,230,000 at the last count. That is about one-fifth of all the people in the world. About 14 million babies are born every year – enough to fill a major city the size of New York.

Missing brother

The Marx brothers were a comedy team of real brothers who made many popular films in the 1930s. Three or four of them appeared in the films, but there was a fifth. They were Chico (real name Leonard), Harpo (Arthur), Groucho (Julius), Zeppo (Herbert), and Gummo (Milton), who never acted in a film.

Your skin helps to keep you cool by sweating salty water. On an average day, you sweat about half a pint (.2l), but on a very hot day you can lose as much as 6 pints (2.8l) of sweat.

Bird bath

Some birds have a bath, carefully washing and cleaning their feathers. Ducks dip down into the water. Other birds stand in a shallow pool of water or have a shower in the rain. Some birds don't get wet at all. They cover themselves with dust and shake it through their feathers, probably to get rid of lice.

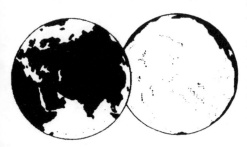

Planet Ocean

Earth is not really the right name for our world. It should be called Ocean because nearly three-quarters of it is covered by water. It has been called the Blue Planet because it looks blue when seen from outer space.

The Trans-Alaska pipeline carries oil from the largest oil field in the United States 800 miles (1,287km) from Prudhoe Bay to the port of Valdez. The oil has to be warmed to keep it from freezing in the pipes.

Horse play

In prehistoric times, there was a breed of horses called eohippus. They were only about the size of a cat.

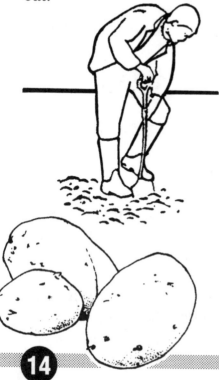

First fries

Potatoes were first grown for food in Peru and Bolivia, South America, more than 1,800 years ago. The Spaniards brought them to Europe in the sixteenth century as an ornamental plant. A few years later, they were grown for food and soon became popular. There are more than 150 varieties.

The oldest known living thing in the world is a bristlecone pine tree. Growing high up in the White Mountains in California, one tree is reckoned to be 4,600 years old and could live for another 600 years.

First ballpoint

The ballpoint pen was invented more than 60 years ago by a Hungarian journalist, Laszlo Bíró, who lived in Argentina. He began making the pens in the 1950s. Now millions are sold every day.

Hop it!

Australia's red kangaroos can travel 42 feet (12.8m) in one huge leap. Using their powerful hind legs and holding their small front paws against their chests, they can hop at speeds of up to 40 mph (64.3km/ph) over short distances. They hold up their tails for balance.

A hole in the Arizona desert is almost 1 mile (1.6km) across and over 500 feet (152m) deep. It was made by a huge meteorite, weighing up to 2 million tons (1.8 million metric tons), which hit Earth 20,000 years ago.

Not so extinct?

Some scientists believe that some types of dinosaurs are still alive today. They developed from the early creatures into the birds we now know.

Printing money

Monopoly™ is a popular board game which involves buying and selling houses and hotels. In 1975, twice as much Monopoly™ money as real money was printed in the United States.

The saguaro is the world's biggest cactus. It grows up to 60 feet (18.3m) high in Arizona and Mexico and can hold up to 4 tons (3.6 metric tons) of water. It shrinks in the dry season and fills out again after rain.

Wacky weights

An average woman weighs about the same as 134 rats. A six-year-old child weighs roughly the same as the air in a small bedroom that is 9 x 9 x 8 feet (2.7 x 2.7 x 2.4m).

How many Strads?

Thousands of violins have labels saying they were made by the famous Italian maker, Antonio Stradivari. But most of them are copies – some very bad copies. Stradivari lived to be 93 and was making violins up to the last year of his life. It is thought he made more than 1,100 violins, violas, and cellos – about 600 survive.

There are more than 15,000 different types of flies in the United States, but little is known about many of them. One type, the downlooker fly, stands head down on tree trunks. No one knows what it feeds on.

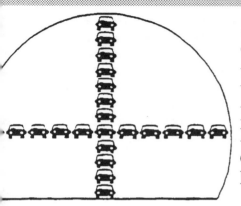

Huge tunnel

One of the largest tunnels in the world burrows under Yerba Buena Island in San Francisco. It is about 11 cars wide and 12 cars high.

Moon flight

The Moon is about a quarter the size of Earth. Flying once around the Moon is about the same as flying from New York to London and back again. One trip around Earth equals four journeys around the Moon.

Have you ever noticed that you breathe more quickly after you have eaten a big meal? This is because you need more energy to digest the food in your stomach, and breathing more quickly helps supply it.

Self-defense

About 200 years ago, an English scientist, Edward Jenner, discovered that giving someone the mild illness cowpox protected them from the serious one called smallpox.

Lobster lines

At the end of each summer, spiny lobsters leave their homes among the rocks and coral beds. They move to another part of the ocean to avoid the great sea storms. They line up in columns of about 70 lobsters. Then they march off at about 18 feet (5.5m) a minute. They walk across the ocean bed all day and night until they find a safer spot to live.

When water freezes into ice, it gets bigger. It also gets lighter and floats on water. If ice did not float, all the seas in the world would have turned to solid ice and nothing would be able to live on Earth.

Swordplay

Kendo is a traditional Japanese martial art based on the skills of the Samurai sword fighters. Today's combatants challenge each other with hollow bamboo poles.

King gone

Richard I, known as Richard the Lion Heart, was king of England for nine years. He spent only six months in England, spending the rest of the time fighting the French and going on crusades to the Holy Land.

A dog can hear a range of sounds – from quiet to loud – two and a half times greater than that heard by humans. A human can make a range of sounds nearly twice as great.

Green giants

Trees are the tallest of all living things. A Californian redwood grows up to 366 feet (111.5m) tall – as high as 63 men.

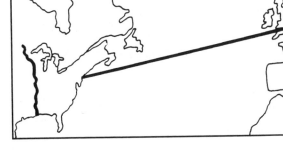

Not so short 'n' curly

If the bends of the Mississippi were straightened out, the river would be longer than the distance from New York to London. Most maps make the Mississippi look shorter than its 3,710-mile (5,970.5km) length.

In 1946, an earthquake under the Pacific Ocean caused a huge tidal wave. It travelled more than 2,000 miles (3,218 km) at a speed of nearly 500 mph (804.6km/ph). When it reached Hawaii, the waves were higher than a three-story house.

Demon dragons

Do not confuse a dragon with a wyvern. Dragons have animal bodies. Wyverns have birds' feet and snakes' bodies.

High-speed sneeze

Did you know that when you sneeze, air and tiny particles of mucus are blown out of your nose at a speed of 100 mph (160.9km/ph)?

No brakes

Some of the world's largest oil tankers, such as the Japanese *Seawise Giant*, weigh up to 645 tons (585 metric tons) when fully loaded. They are so heavy that when the captain orders the ship to stop, it takes up to 4 miles (6.4km) to come to a standstill.

The world's largest seed looks like a giant coconut and can weigh up to 40 lb (18kg). It comes from the nut palms which grow only on the Seychelles Islands. Some nuts fall into the sea and float for thousands of miles.

Drawing with puff

An airbrush has no bristles, and it is not a brush. It is a tube the size of a ballpoint pen. Air blowing through it forces a fine spray of paint from the nozzle.

Long and tall

The French supertanker *Bellamya* is 1,320 feet (402.3m) long. That is 62 feet 4 inches (18.9m) longer than the Empire State Building in New York, without its mast.

The Sahara, the biggest desert in the world, is almost as large as the United States. Until about 4,000 years ago it was covered with grass and was the home of buffalo, elephants, lions, and antelopes.

Deadly weapon

A bolas spider sets to work making a weapon to kill its prey as soon as night falls. First, it spins a single thread and crawls to the middle of it. Then it carefully makes another thread on which it hangs a ball of spider silk. When the spider swings the thread, the weight of the ball helps to wind the thread around the prey so it cannot escape.

There are about 1,500 different blends of tea. The Chinese and Japanese have drunk tea for thousands of years. The leaves were first taken to Europe about 400 years ago.

Three in one

A mythical creature, the griffin, had a lion's body, the wings of a bird, and the head of an eagle.

Mysterious explosion

On June 30, 1908, something from outer space hit Earth in a remote part of northern Siberia. No one really knows what it was – only that it was a huge fireball. It was so powerful that it melted metal objects and burned herds of reindeer. The blast from it uprooted trees and blew people to the ground.

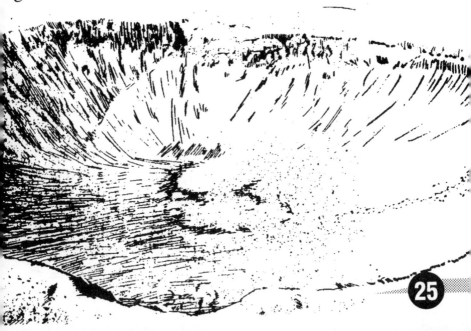

About three-quarters of all the fresh water in the world is frozen in the Arctic and Antarctic ice caps. If they melted, the sea levels would rise by 200 feet (60.9m) and New York, London, and Paris would be under water.

Ballet terms

Ballet, from the French word *bal* meaning dance, developed from spectacles of music and dance performed in Italian and French courts. Until 1681 professionals were all male and wore masks. In the eighteenth century, French ballet was adopted by other countries, so the French terms stuck and are still used today.

1 *Arabesque*
2 *Attitude*
3 *Fouette*
4 *Pas de deux*
5 *Pirouette*

Heaven made

The Hindu god Brahma is often shown with four faces and four arms, representing aspects of the Hindu faith.

The world's first oil well was drilled in Pennsylvania in 1859 by a retired railroad guard called Edwin Drake. Since then, about one-third of all the known oil in the world has been used up.

Underwater whistling

Whales communicate with each other underwater by making whistling, clicking, and moaning sounds. These strange noises, which may be very loud, can be picked up by other whales hundreds of miles away. Male and female whales also leap out of the water and kiss each other. Dolphins too, make sounds, including groans, barks, and squeals. With these noises, whales and dolphins "talk" to each other in languages of their own.

Someone living in a Western country walks about 50,000 miles (80,450km) in a lifetime. Shoes on the right foot usually wear out faster than shoes on the left foot. Why this is, no one knows.

Powerful poison

The poison-arrow frog, which lives in Colombia, is the world's most poisonous creature. One frog has enough poison to kill about 2,200 people.

Building without rooms

Three thousand years ago, the peoples of the Middle East built huge brick temples for their gods. The buildings were solid and in layers, but over the years they have worn away and now look like pyramids.

When the first American telegraph systems were set up, the poles holding up the wires were often pushed over. The herds of wild bison used these poles as rubbing and scratching posts.

Raindrops

For every drop of rain that falls on Cairo in Egypt, there are 23 times more drops falling in London in Britain. In Guinea, on the west coast of Africa, the capital of Conakry has on average more rain each year than any other capital city in the world. The rainfall is 170 times heavier than in Cairo and 7 times heavier than in London. The least rain falls on the Atacama Desert in Chile. There was no rain at all for 400 years and now the record is still nil.

Conakry   **London**

Cairo

Fishermen in Papua New Guinea use spiders' webs as fishing nets. Tropical orb spiders spin webs up to 8 feet (2.4m) across between trees. The fishermen scoop up the web on a loop of stick and catch fish up to 1 lb (453gm) in weight.

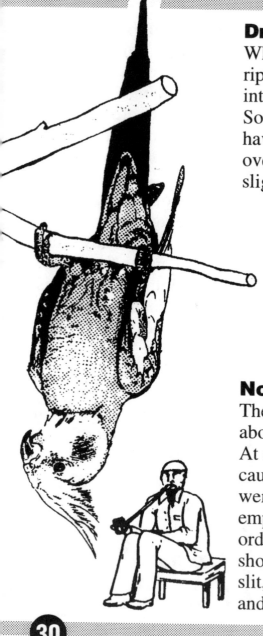

Drunk on cherries

When fruit gets over-ripe, the juice can turn into a kind of alcohol. Some fruit-eating birds have been known to eat overripe cherries and get slightly drunk.

No smoking!

There is nothing new about a ban on smoking. At one time, Turks caught smoking tobacco were put to death. The emperor of Russia ordered that smokers should have their noses slit, then be whipped and sent off to Siberia.

On National Fly-Catching Day in Tokyo, Japan, in 1933, the official count of flies killed was over 117,000,000. Even without a big swat, flies have short lives – females about 29 days, males about 17 days.

Fiery fortunes

The ancient Greeks believed they could tell someone's fortune by staring into the flames of a fire. Some thought the future could be seen in the ashes of a fire that burned a personal possession.

Jumping joeys

Many young animals have names that are different from their parents'. A baby kangaroo is called a joey.

Bison are so big and heavy, they can fight off wolves and are not frightened by them. Native Americans wore clothes made of wolf skins when hunting bison because they could get close without scaring the animals away.

Racing past

The marathon race is named after a flat area in Greece where the ancient Persians and Greeks fought a battle. A messenger raced from the battlefield of Marathon 25 miles (40.2km) to Athens with the news of the Greek victory.

The Great Pyramid

The pyramids of Egypt are the only survivors of what the ancient Greeks called the Seven Wonders of the World. They are still wonders. The oldest, the Great Pyramid, was built as a tomb for the pharaoh Khufu, who died over 4,500 years ago. It contains more than two million blocks of stone. Some weigh 15 tons (13.6 metric tons) – as much as four small cars.

There are more than 3,000 cubic miles (12,500 cubic km) of water in Earth's atmosphere. It is reckoned that if it all fell as rain at the same time, the whole world would be covered with 1 inch (2.5cm) of water.

Tall tales

A bear-like creature, called a megathere, which lived in prehistoric times, was 20 feet (6.09m) high – over three times as tall as an average man.

Golden sheets

Gold is so soft that a lump the size of a matchbox can be flattened out into a sheet big enough to cover a tennis court.

Bread was used as a plate in the Middle Ages. Thick slices of bread, called trenchers, were loaded with meats and other foods for a feast. After the feast, the fatty, soggy trenchers were given to the poor.

Tall stories

The Great Pyramid of Khufu at Giza in Egypt is 175 feet 11 inches (53.6m) taller than the Statue of Liberty in New York, which is 305 feet (93m). The Eiffel Tower in Paris is taller than both of them at 1,052 feet 4 inches (320.7m).

When you dive into water, your heartbeat slows down. This is one of your body's survival tricks. It slows down the effect of the lack of oxygen on your body and helps you to hold your breath longer.

Fooling your foes

Many flies are eaten by other creatures, such as spiders and birds. The lantern fly of Southeast Asia confuses its enemies because it has markings on its rear end that look like a head. Which way is this one walking? Answer: to the left.

Star names

Many actors choose star-like names for themselves. Marilyn Monroe, the famous film star, was born Norma Jean Mortenson (later Baker). She adopted the more memorable name when she began acting in films in 1948.

Squirrel monkeys sometimes leap high out of the trees where they live to snatch flying insects from the air. They may reach a height of more than 60 feet (18.3m) above the treetops.

Name of a dog

A tax collector, called Louis Dobermann, lived in Germany about 120 years ago. He was not welcome when he came to collect money. To protect him, he bred large fierce dogs. They became known as Doberman pinschers and are still used as guard dogs today.

Poles apart

About 600 million years ago, all the world's land was joined together. It slowly split up into today's continents.

Smallest fish

The Marshall Islands goby is the smallest-known fish in the world. Just over one-half inch (1.3cm) long, one would fit on your thumbnail.

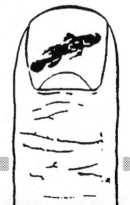

Some people grow huge fruits and vegetables. The largest recorded cabbage weighed 114 lb (51.7kg), the largest tomato weighed over 4 lb (1.8kg), and the largest pumpkin weighed 377 lb (171kg).

Walking arch

The Marble Arch in London, Britain, was built outside Buckingham Palace. Because it was too narrow for the royal coach to go through, it was moved more than 100 years ago to its present site near Hyde Park and Oxford Street.

Bugs alive

If you lived 100 million years ago, you may have met an arthropleura. This insect, 6 feet (1.8m) long, lived on forest floors.

A hero shrew has the strongest backbone of any animal in proportion to its size. Its backbone protects it from being crushed when it burrows in the ground. It is said a person can stand on a shrew without harming it.

Full up

At least 12 Greyhound buses would be needed to carry the 500 passengers and crew of just one Boeing 747 jumbo jet.

KO'd by a kangaroo

Rival male kangaroos fight each other with punch-like strokes. When a kangaroo escaped from a Japanese circus, it knocked out three men but was stopped by two policemen with judo skills.

St. Pantaleone was once the patron saint of Venice in Italy. He was later depicted in a play as a silly old man who wore long trousers. From the play, trousers were called pantaloons, later shortened to "pants."

Special spirals

About 100 million years ago, the female dinosaur Protoceratops would lay 12 or more eggs in a sandy hollow nest. She would place them carefully in a spiral with all the narrow ends of the eggs pointing inward.

Chameleons, which are a type of lizard, get their name from two Greek words meaning "ground lion." This is a strange name because all chameleons, except one rare kind, live in trees.

Sleepwalker

The famous French racing driver, Alain Prost, sometimes walks in his sleep. Once he woke up to find himself on a roof!

On track for victory

A Civil War gun was mounted on a railroad car so that it could be moved quickly around the country.

The first escalator in Britain was put in Harrods department store in 1898. An attendant waited at the top and handed a glass of brandy to any customer who was upset by the ride.

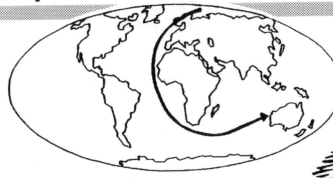

Terrific tern

An arctic tern was found in Freemantle, Western Australia. It had flown halfway around the world – 12,000 miles (19,311km) – from a bird sanctuary on the White Sea coast in Russia.

Barber's striped pole

Men used to go to a barber's shop for a haircut. Each shop had a red-and-white striped pole outside. This was because barbers used to "bleed" people. They cut a person's arm and let it bleed. This was thought to cure some illnesses. Barbers wrapped the used bandages around a pole and left it outside as a sign that they would bleed people.

Stapelia flowers smell like rotting meat, and the leaves look like the skin of a dead animal. This attracts flies that feed on decaying flesh. The hungry flies then pollinate the flowers.

Banned for drinking lemonade

In 1898, a professional boxer fought an amateur boxer in a match in Copenhagen. After the match, the amateur boxer accepted a glass of lemonade from the professional. The amateur was then banned from amateur boxing for having made "material gain" from a fight.

A fire has been burning in Australia for about 2,000 years. It started when a seam of coal in New South Wales was set on fire, perhaps by lightning. The fire is now 500 feet (152.4km) below the ground.

Bigger than a car

Saltwater crocodiles in Northern Australia grow up to 20 feet long (6.1m) – that is longer than a car.

Sharing your bed

Did you know that every night you share your bed with lots of other creatures? Dust mites are so small you can't see them, but there are billions in every house. About a million live in a single bed, munching away on flakes of human skin that rub off all the time. Bedbugs are much bigger, and you know when they are with you. They bite and suck blood.

The Statue of Liberty in New York Harbor was built by a Frenchman, Gustave Eiffel – famous for the Eiffel Tower in Paris. Finished in 1886, the statue was a gift from the French people to the Americans.

Smallest bird

This is the actual size of Helena's hummingbird from Cuba – the smallest bird in the world.

Tribolite eyes

Tribolites were the first animals to have eyes. Some of them had as many as 20,000 lenses in each eye. Human beings have only one. Tribolites lived in the sea millions of years ago and looked a little like wood lice. They became extinct about 230 million years ago, but you can see their fossil remains in many museums around the world.

Each American eats an average of 40 pints (18.8l) of ice cream every year. That is about five times more than the average Briton. The world's largest ice cream was a sundae made in Iowa. It weighed more than 2 tons (1.8 metric tons).

Hard workers

Hummingbirds are very busy birds.
If you worked at the same rate as a hummingbird, you would have to drink almost your own weight in water every hour just to keep cool. And you would have to eat almost twice your weight in food to get enough energy.

Bumps on the head

More than a hundred years ago, a popular way of finding out a person's character was by "reading" the bumps on his head. The shape of his skull and its uneven surface were believed to show all a person's abilities, attitudes, personality, and even if he was likely to be a poet, a drunkard, or a criminal.

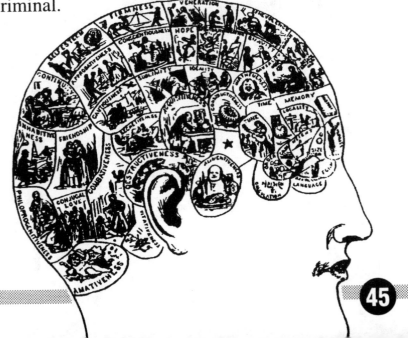

The world's slowest animal is a three-toed sloth. On the ground, it moves at a speed of about 6 feet (1.8m) a minute. It is a little faster in the trees, where it sleeps for 18 hours a day.

Jumping jacks

The gravity of some planets is much less than Earth's gravity. Using the force you need to jump 3 feet (.9m) on Earth, you would leap 9 feet (2.7m) on Mercury.

Inner secrets

Over 3,000 years ago, people tried to learn about their futures by "reading" animal intestines. The head of the giant Humbaba (an ancient Assyrian divination figure) was sculpted to look as though it were made of intestines.

When the first railroads were built in Europe, more than 150 years ago, experts thought that human beings could not travel faster than 20 mph (32.1km/ph). The theory was that at speeds over that, their bodies would explode.

Lucky mothers
Horses have one baby at a time, but pigs give birth to an average of nine babies at a time.

What a stinker!
In 1970, an international competition was abandoned because it was thought to be too dangerous for anyone but the Swedes. The competitors had to eat rotten herrings.

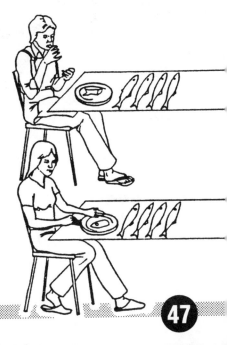

You can draw a line nearly 15 miles (24.1km) long with one ordinary pencil. But the lead in a pencil is not made of lead. It is a mixture of clay and a black mineral called graphite.

Tunnels in trees

Some weaver birds build very unusual nests of reeds in trees. A long entrance tunnel leads to the main part of the nest. This protects the eggs and chicks from hungry predators.

One-piece suit

Ancient Romans wore a garment called a toga. It was a large half circle of woolen cloth which they wrapped around themselves in a special way.

Future dreams

Some people believe that if you dream of climbing up a ladder or stairs, you will be successful. Dreaming of going downstairs means your future will be full of failures and disappointments.

The whistling thorn tree gets its name from the strange music it makes. Some of the balls on the tree have holes made by ants. When the wind blows across the holes, the tree "whistles."

Pennies for heaven

Six hundred years ago, if you wanted to go to heaven when you died, you simply bought a certificate, called an indulgence, from the Catholic Church in Rome.

A cheetah is the fastest animal in the world. It has a top speed of 80 mph (128.7km/ph) but only over a short distance. After about 500 yards (457m), it gets hot and breathless and has to lie down for a rest.

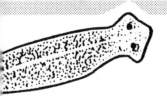

Splitting up

Flatworms don't have to go to the trouble of having babies. After mating, they just split into two new worms. Each one is then both a father and mother.

What a spectacle!

Bifocal glasses, which have special lenses for reading and for seeing distant objects, were invented by the eighteenth-century American statesman Benjamin Franklin.

Pitcher plants feed on insects and even scorpions and lizards. Attracted by sweet nectar, the insects fall into the plant's round, hollow leaves and drown in a pool of liquid at the bottom.

Good dad

A king penguin chick takes 60 days to hatch out of its egg. During this time, the male penguin stands on the Antarctic ice, cradling the egg on its feet and keeping it warm under a flap of soft feathers.

Harder than diamond

Diamond is the hardest known natural substance in the world. It can scratch every other material. The only thing that will scratch a diamond is called borazon. It is made up of boron and nitrogen.

Hundreds and even thousands of prairie dogs live in one huge underground burrow, or "town." Each family has its own part. A sentry at each entrance to the burrow warns of approaching danger.

Fiery breath

A 200-year-old cannon was made in the shape of a sitting tiger.

Kitchen concert

By holding two spoons in one hand, you can clack them to play a tune.

Squirting cucumbers spread their seeds by firing them out of their fruits. The fruits split open and the seeds shoot out at a speed of more than 60 mph (96.5km/ph) and land up to 26 feet (7.9m) away from the plant.

Spider giant

The giant spider crab has a claw span of 12 feet 1 inch (3.7m). Here it is measured against a 17-foot-long (5.2m) canoe.

Lucky aces?

If you have your fortune told with cards, hope that you are dealt the ace of clubs, which means wealth, health, love, and happiness. The ace of spades can mean death.

In winter, reindeer scrape away the thick layer of snow to find green lichen, or "moss," underneath it. Reindeer need more than 20 lb (9kg) of this food every day to stay alive.

Anything goes

Birds will build their nests out of almost anything. Some use their own saliva, while others collect mud, sheep's wool, spiders' webs, feathers, moss, or pebbles. A crested flycatcher uses old snakeskins.

Zombies

Sleepwalkers cannot hear sounds, taste, or smell anything. They only remember what they have done as if they have dreamed about it.

There are more than 8,000 different types of ants in the world. Most of them live in huge colonies in hot, tropical countries. One colony might have as many as 200,000 ants in it but only one egg-laying queen.

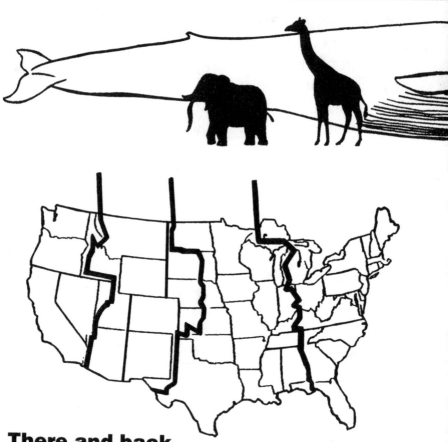

There and back

America is divided into different time zones. From east to west, each zone is one hour behind. If you leave for school at 9:15 A.M. and walk east to west for 15 minutes across a time zone boundary, you would arrive at 8:30 A.M. – 45 minutes before you set off! The same walk home would take 1 hour and 15 minutes!

Nearly 16,000 men died in the first attempt to build the Panama Canal. After nine years, the canal was abandoned, mainly because swarms of mosquitoes gave the workers malaria and yellow fever.

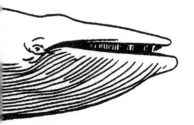

What a whopper!

The largest animal on Earth is the blue whale. Females are bigger than males and weigh about 110 tons (99.7 metric tons). On dry land, the heaviest animal is a male elephant, and a male giraffe is the tallest.

Giant waves

The highest waves ever recorded were in an Alaskan bay. Some were more than 1,740 feet (530.3m) tall – higher than the Empire State Building in New York.

Hyenas hunt at night in packs of about 30. They can run down large animals, which they attack with their sharp teeth. Their usual call is a long howl, but when excited they make a cackling noise.

Pole arms

Pole arms were sharp metal blades and spikes attached to the ends of long poles. Foot soldiers used them before the invention of guns. Here are some fierce examples.

Plankton – a tiny plant that lives in seawater – produces flashes of light. If there is enough of one type of plankton, the light can be bright enough for you to read a book.

Big bones

This man is standing beside the fossilized leg bone, a femur, of a dinosaur. No one knew that the dinosaurs existed until about 150 years ago. When these bones were first found, people thought they were the bones of giant men.

Man against car

From a standing start, a man could beat a modern racing car for about 30 feet (9.1m).

A giant anteater swallows thousands of ants or termites for one meal. It tears open the insects' nest with its long claws, pushes in its tongue – nearly 2 feet (.6m) long – and picks up hundreds of insects.

Ancient temple

The Parthenon, a ruined marble temple stands high on a hill in Athens, Greece. It was the temple of Athena Parthenos, Athena the maiden. The Turks occupied Athens in the 1400s and used the Parthenon as a gunpowder store. It blew up in 1687 and wrecked the temple.

Unique you

No two people have exactly the same fingerprints. This means your fingerprints are different from the fingerprints of all the 5,000 million other people in the world.

Ivy and other climbing plants cling onto walls and trees using tiny roots growing on their stems. The plants only use the trees for support and do not harm them.

Handwalking

Skunks ward off attackers by turning their backs, standing on their front legs, and spraying the enemy with a really foul-smelling liquid.

Whirling weapon

About a hundred years ago in India, Sikhs used a "frisbee" type of weapon. They twirled a razor-sharp metal quoit on one finger and hurled it at the enemy.

Bushbabies hunt for food at night. They have such good hearing that when they sleep during the day, they fold up their ears to cover their ear holes. This stops the noises of the forest from keeping them awake.

Skyscraper
One of the tallest sunflowers ever measured was 23 feet 6 inches (7.2m) high.

Great grabbers!
Alexander the Great, who lived about 2,300 years ago, ordered all his soldiers to shave their heads and faces. This prevented an enemy from grabbing a soldier by the hair to cut his head off.

Deadly kiss
Cuttlefish, a type of octopus, mate and then both die before their eggs hatch.

Velcro is made of nylon. One strip is covered with tiny hooks; the other has tiny loops. When the two strips are pressed together, the hooks catch onto the loops, and the two strips stick together.

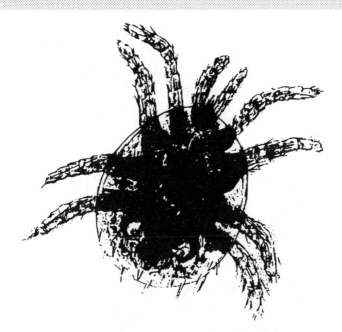

Bee's knees

The creature above has been magnified 100 times. It is really only 1 mm long. It lives on a bee's knees – the bee on the left is shown at its actual size.

Moles keep underground larders of living worms. When a mole finds worms in its tunnel, it eats as many as it can. It then bites the leftovers on their backs to stop them from sliding away.

Skybaby

One of the smallest fully flying planes, the Stits Skybaby, has a wingspan of just 7 feet 2 inches (2.2m). It is shown here against a Boeing 747 jet engine.

Toothless terror

The dunkleosteus lived over 300 million years ago. Even without teeth, this 30-foot (9.1m) fish was a threat to all sea creatures.

When a housefly has finished its meal, it flies off and vomits its food. Then it eats it again. The dirty spots you see on windows are the fly's vomit. It often carries germs that can spread diseases.

Finger power
Warren L. Travis is reported to have lifted 667 lb (302.5kg) with one finger – the equivalent of lifting four men.

Heaven and hell
Westminster Cathedral in London, Britain, was built on land that was once the site of a prison and a fairground. A former prison, Alcatraz in San Francisco Bay, is now a tourist attraction.

A hippopotamus has huge teeth, but it only eats plants. A female hippo uses her teeth to fight off crocodiles who try to attack her calf. A male hippo uses his teeth to fight other males.

Man on the Moon

Since the first landing by Neil Armstrong on July 20, 1969, 17 other men have walked on the Moon. So far, no woman has had the chance for a stroll.

Tiny tots

This is the actual size of a pygmy shrew. It is 3 inches (7.6cm) from its nose to the end of its tail.

Plants have roots to hold them in the ground and to absorb water and food from the soil. The roots of wheat plants produce slime. This helps the root to slide through the soil as it grows downwards.

Spinning around

Cyclones bring stormy weather. The air in a cyclone spins around and towards its center. Cyclones in the northern half of the world move in a counterclockwise direction. In the southern half, they move in a clockwise direction. This is caused by Earth's spinning on its axis.

Be warned

The Etruscans, who lived long ago in Italy, believed Tin, the god of thunder, sent them warnings to mend their ways. After two warnings, they would be struck by a thunderbolt.

Insects make buzzing noises by beating their wings very fast. The faster they beat their wings, the higher the sound. A mosquito makes a high-pitched whine by flapping its wings about 600 times a second.

100 goals

Native Americans used to play a ball game like baseball. It had up to 600 players, and they were often badly hurt or even killed. The game lasted until 100 goals had been scored.

Legging it

Some creepy-crawlies have lots of legs.
1 Caterpillars usually have 8.
2 "Centipede" means 100 feet, but some centipedes have 354 legs.
3 "Millipede" means 1,000 feet, but the largest recorded number of feet on a millipede is 710.

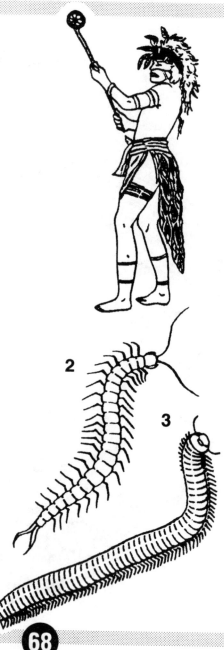

The best and most expensive wool for clothes doesn't come from sheep but from goats. Cashmere is made from Kashmir goats which live in northern India and Tibet. Mohair is made with the wool of Angora goats.

Meteor attack

Over 75 million meteors bombard Earth every day. Most are the size of a pinhead (**a**), and some the size of a grape (**b**). Nearly all of them burn up in Earth's atmosphere.

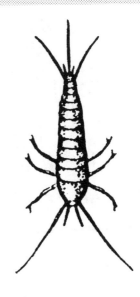

Wrong name

A silverfish is not made of silver and is not a fish. It is a tiny insect that lives in houses, eating anything with paste or glue on it.

Half full

Over half of our bodies are water. Men have slightly more water than women.

A large American possum plays dead when it is attacked. It lies still with its mouth open and eyes staring. If the enemy goes away, it takes a quick look around and comes back to life.

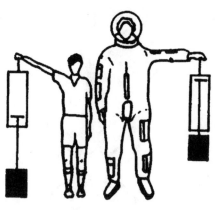

Weighty matters

A bucket of sand on the Moon would weigh about a sixth of what it would weigh on Earth. This is because Earth's gravity is six times stronger than the Moon's.

Not a tapestry

The Bayeux Tapestry is a 230-foot (70m) strip of linen. Its pictures tell the story of the Norman invasion of Britain in 1066. A real tapestry has pictures woven into the fabric. The Bayeux Tapestry is not a real tapestry. It is a piece of embroidery – linen embroidered with wool.

Birch trees produce tiny grains of yellow pollen. One spike may have over five million grains on it. Blown by the wind, the grains land on other birch trees. They pollinate the flowers so the tree can produce seeds.

Faster than a horse

Jesse Owens was a great American athlete who competed in the long jump and in hurdles and who played basketball. He once beat a horse in a 100-yard (91.4m) race.

Mighty midget

This is the actual size of a pistol. It has two barrels and two bullets. If you missed the first time, you got a second chance.

Mojave squirrels dig tunnels up to 20 feet (6.1m) long and 3 feet (.9m) deep in the desert. Away from the heat, they sleep for up to five days a week through the dry winters when there is little food.

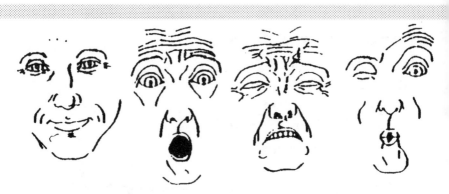

Facing up to it

Our faces show many emotions – surprise, fear, pleasure, and so on. Look in the mirror. How many different expressions can you make?

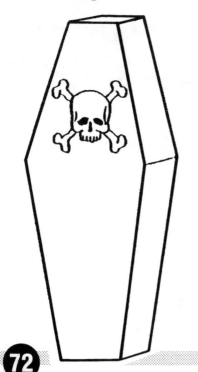

Day of the Dead

The Day of the Dead is a festival held in Mexico each year. It celebrates death, and people have parties around graves, eating chocolates and candy in the shape of skeletons and coffins. In Mexican Indian folklore, the dead return to life on this day.

Potato chips are made by cutting potatoes into very thin slices and frying them in oil. In the chips are tiny pockets of air. When you bite a chip, the crunching sound is the pockets of air exploding.

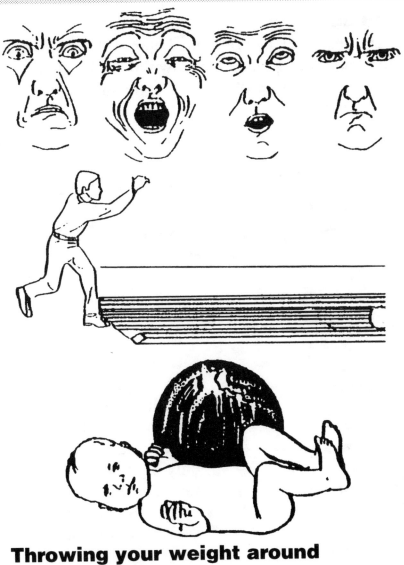

Throwing your weight around

A bowling ball weighs just about the same as an average six-month-old baby – 16 lb (7.3kg).

There are about 1,800 different kinds of fleas in the world. They live on the blood of people, birds, and other animals. Most kinds of fleas prefer one type of animal but will feed on anything if really hungry.

End up

If 26 tiles, each showing one letter of the alphabet, were randomly placed facedown, there would be a 1 in 15,600 chance of turning up the last three to spell "end."

Guardian ants

Bullhorn acacia trees in Central America have a special link with ants. Some kinds of ant live only on these thorny trees and feed on their nectar. In return, the ants drive off insects and larger animals that try to eat the acacias.

Huge chunks of ice break off the ends of glaciers in the Antarctic and float away as icebergs. The biggest iceberg ever recorded was in 1956. It covered about 11,900 square miles (30,702 sq km) – almost as big as Maryland.

Easier to look happy

It takes more than 40 muscles to frown but only 17 to put a smile on your face.

Shrinking water

If you put two spoonfuls of sugar in a glass of water, the water level goes down. This is because the liquid becomes denser and takes up less space.

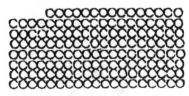

Turned turtle

A female green turtle lays an average of 1,800 eggs in her life. Of these, 1,395 don't hatch, 374 hatch but quickly die, and only 3 live long enough to breed.

Trade rats got their name because they steal shiny things during the night and leave a small rock or twig in their place. There is a story that one trade rat ran off with a lighted candle.

Half-brained

Did you know that your brain has two halves, called hemispheres? The right one controls the left side of your body, and the left one controls the right side of your body.

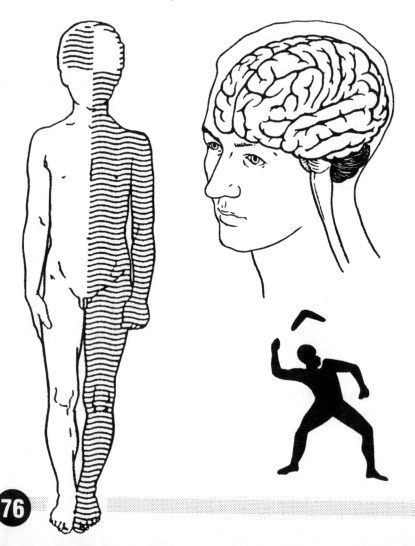

The biggest natural sponge ever found was one called Neptune's cup. It was over 3 feet (.9m) long. More than 4,000 different types of sponge grow in the Mediterranean Sea and around the West Indian coasts.

Razor-teeth fish

Piranhas are terrifying fish. They have rows of razor-sharp teeth and strong jaws. They live in South American rivers and will attack shoals of fish, cattle, and even human beings.

Carved in stone

Wind, rain, and frost wear away rocks and stones into strange shapes, like natural carvings.

Booming boomerangs

Aborigines living in Australia are so good at throwing their wooden boomerangs, they can kill an animal as far away as 500 feet (152.4m) with one.

You have about 62,000 miles (99,200km) of blood vessels in your body. Some are as thick as your forefinger and some as thin as a hair. If they were all stretched out in one line, they would go around the world twice.

Extinct birds that couldn't fly

1 The New Zealand giant moa, the tallest bird, was 11 feet 6 inches (3.5m) tall.

2 The Madagascan elephant bird, the heaviest bird, weighed 970 lb (440kg).

3 The North American "terror crane" was 6 feet 6 inches (1.9m) tall.

4 The largest South American bird was 6 feet 6 inches (1.9m) high.

Seasick seaman

Horatio Lord Nelson was one of Britain's greatest admirals, but he was often seasick for the first few days of a voyage.

A bull moose has the biggest antlers of all deer. They can grow up to 6 feet (1.8m) wide. The antlers are covered with furry skin, called velvet, which a moose rubs off against trees.

Deadly beauty

The Pacific Ocean lionfish eats small fish alive. It is also dangerous to human beings because its spikes have poisonous tips.

3

4

Angel Falls in Venezuela got its name from Jimmy Angel, an American pilot who flew over it in 1936. It is the world's highest waterfall: the river drops 3,212 feet (979m) down the side of Devil Mountain.

Strange serpent

This old musical horn is called a serpent. Made of wood, it has six finger holes. Some serpents were more than 6.5 feet (1.9m) long. They were still played in military bands and in churches until about 100 years ago.

An elephant has the biggest ear flaps of any animal in the world. An African elephant's ears – about 6 feet (1.8m) across – are larger than an Indian elephant's. It flaps them to cool itself down.

The truth about Frankenstein

Frankenstein was not a real person or a monster. In Mary Shelley's book, *Frankenstein*, he was a scientist who created a monster from parts of dead men. So the monster was not Frankenstein but Frankenstein's monster.

The oldest known bird is a royal albatross called "Grandma." She is about 66 years old. Most small birds die before they are a year old. They are killed by other birds, animals, cars, and diseases.

Pedal power

This is the actual size of the world's smallest bike. It was made in Australia in 1974, and its wheels are only 1.25 inches (3.2cm) across.

The only known vampire moth lives in Malaysia. It pushes its long, sharp mouth tube through the skin of buffalo, tapirs, and other mammals and sucks their blood for up to an hour at each feed.

No reverse gear

Sharks are fierce hunters. But, unlike most fish, they have no swim bladders (a kind of buoyancy tank) to keep them afloat. To keep from sinking, they have to be on the move all the time. A shark can swim up and down and turn quickly but cannot swim backwards, like most fish.

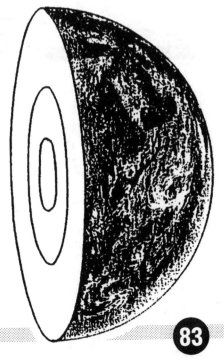

Hot center

If you could cut Earth in half, you would see it has several layers. The nearer each layer is to the center, the hotter it is. At the center, the temperature is 7,600°F (4,205°C) – a hundred times hotter than a warm day.

People were making music over 20,000 years ago. They played flutes made of reindeer antlers and bear bones. They made whistles from hollow bird bones and the toe bones of deer.

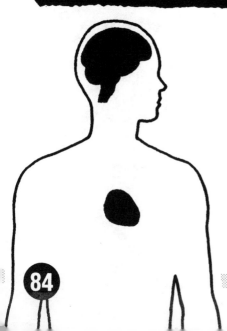

Watchful eyes

A honeybee has five eyes. Two of the eyes have a large number of lenses.

Massive weight

A neutron star is very heavy. Only the size of a pinhead, it weighs as much as a huge ocean liner.

Brainy

Your brain weighs about three times as much as your heart.

The bird with the most feathers in the world is a whistling swan. It has more than 25,000. The bird with the fewest feathers is a ruby-throated hummingbird. It has only 940.

Smallest flower

The artillery flower of India is the smallest known flower in the world. Each bloom is only 0.35 mm (less than a tenth of an inch) across. More than 20 blooms would fit inside this O.

Non-starter

This monocycle was designed by an American over 100 years ago. The rider sits inside the single wheel and pedals it along. It was not a success.

Without green plants, we would all die. Green plants produce all the oxygen that we need to breathe. In sunlight, these plants take in carbon dioxide gas and turn it into oxygen.

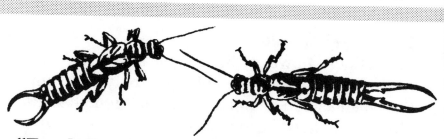

"Ear-ie" creepy-crawlies

Earwigs are small brown insects with pincers on their rear ends. They got their name from an old superstition – people believed they crawled inside a sleeping person's ears and made them sick. Earwigs are, in fact, harmless.

Fishy features

When a human baby, an embryo, first starts to develop inside its mother, it looks quite different from when it is born nine months later. In fact, it does not even look human. At four weeks, it has slits near its neck that look a little like the gills of a fish. At six weeks, it still looks fish-like with a tail as well as arms and legs. After a few months, the gills and tail disappear, and the embryo begins to look human.

When the Kariba Dam on the Zambezi River in Zimbabwe began to fill up with water in 1959, there were hundreds of earthquakes. The weight of the water was forcing rocks to shift underground.

Long haul

It took six powerful engines, three pulling and three pushing, to move the world's largest freight train in West Virginia. The 500 coal trucks stretched for 5 miles (8km).

Hopeful mothers

The sunfish holds the record for producing the most eggs. She can lay up to 300 million at one time.

Fleas live on hedgehogs, making their homes among the prickles. Even smaller creatures – so small you can only see them with a microscope – creep between the scales of the fleas.

The dreams of Dickens

Oliver Twist, Mr. Pickwick, Fagin, and many other characters all came from the dreams of the famous author Charles Dickens.

The nails on your fingers and toes grow very slowly – just over 1 inch (2.5cm) in a year. A man in India grew one thumbnail until it was more than 45 inches (114cm) long.

Sweet partnership

The honey guide bird got its name because it guides honey badgers to where honey is stored in a bees' nest in a tree. The honey guide loves eating honey and even beeswax but cannot break into the nest on its own. Chattering loudly, the bird leads a honey badger to a nest. The badger breaks open the honeycombs, and the bird and the animal share a feast.

Flick 'n' lick

A chameleon's tongue is as long as its body. It shoots it out to catch flies.

Sand dunes are always on the move, burying everything that stands in their way. The wind blows the sand up one side of a dune, and the sand slides down the other, slowing moving forward.

Eggstra special

An ostrich lays the largest egg in the world – it is 6–8 inches (15–20cm) long. That is longer than a man's hand. A hummingbird's egg is under half an inch (1.3cm) long.

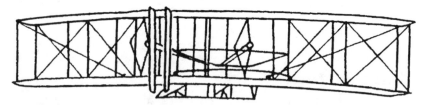

Bicycles to planes

Before making the first airplanes, Orville and Wilbur Wright were bicycle makers. Flyer 1, in which Orville made the first flight, weighed 560 lb (254kg). when empty – 20 times more than a modern racing bicycle.

You can see dark patches on the Moon even without a telescope. Before telescopes were invented, people thought these patches were water and named them "seas." But there is no water on the Moon, and nothing can grow.

Lucky you

You may be lucky or unlucky – it depends on the cat and where you are. A black cat is unlucky in America but lucky in Britain.

Needlework

A tailor bird gets its name from the way it builds its nest. It sews two leaves together, using its beak for a needle and plant fibers for thread.

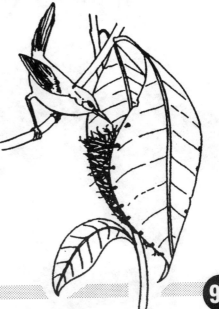

A human has a total of 52 teeth in a lifetime. The first 20 are lost by the age of 13 and are eventually replaced by 32 adult teeth.

Double vision

A rabbit's eyes are positioned so that it can see objects in front of it and behind it at the same time.

Hands on

In ice hockey, a goalkeeper's two gloves are very different from each other. One is for the stick hand and the other for the catching hand.

INDEX